Made in United States
Cleveland, OH
05 March 2025

14918929R00056